POEMS FOR STILLNESS

POEMS FOR STILLNESS

With an introduction by
ANA SAMPSON

Edited by
GABY MORGAN

MACMILLAN COLLECTOR'S LIBRARY

This collection first published 2021 by Macmillan Collector's Library
an imprint of Pan Macmillan
The Smithson, 6 Briset Street, London EC1M 5NR
EU representative: Macmillan Publishers Ireland Limited, Mallard Lodge,
Lansdowne Village, Dublin 4
Associated companies throughout the world
www.panmacmillan.com

ISBN 978-1-5290-4564-2

1 3 5 7 9 8 6 4 2

A CIP catalogue record for this book is available from the British Library.

Cover and endpaper design: Mel Four, Pan Macmillan Art Department
Typeset in Plantin MT Std by Jouve (UK), Milton Keynes
Printed and bound in China by Imago

Visit **www.panmacmillan.com** to read more
about all our books and to buy them.

For Friday Club x

Contents

FRIENDSHIP AND GRATITUDE

PRAYERS AND BLESSINGS

PEACE AND CONSOLATION

Preface

ANA SAMPSON

The world moves quickly – and so do we – but this beautiful collection of poems forms an effective prescription for tranquillity. These verses demonstrate poetry's ability to raise us up. A poet can elevate our thoughts above the humdrum, plucking us out of the scrum of life to set us down somewhere high and quiet, where only gentle winds whistle. No wonder so many sonnets have been composed perched upon peaks: each of these poems offers us an ejector seat and, with that lifting, a true and deeply calming sense of perspective.

Many of the poets in this anthology find their paths to stillness in the natural world, and we can enjoy stepping into the peace of morning with Browning when 'the hillside's dew-pearled'. The remembered splendours of the earth can become a treasure house of wealth that is never spent, to draw upon when needed, like Wordsworth's daffodils, ready to 'flash upon that inward eye'. 'I'll make a summer within my heart', writes Margaret Armour, and so can we. Birds and beasts have lessons for us, too: may we all imitate Lawrence's languorous cat, 'sleeping on the hearth, and yawning before the fire'.

Cool and distant, yet endlessly magnificent, the stars wheel their slow dances many miles above us. Things high and far can make us feel small and quiet in the best possible way. We witness in these pages both a single star lighting Sara Teasdale's solitude in a February twilight, and the multitudes glimpsed by Robert Louis

Stevenson when he flees the nursery after lights out, and both bring a deep sense of peace.

When we cease striving, we are happy. These poets remind us to savour tiny joys, like a child running into the garden after days of rain in Katherine Mansfield's 'A Fine Day'. Wonder can be an engine of tranquillity, too. Walt Whitman writes a hymn to everyday awe, the kind we need to step outside the rushing hours to appreciate: 'every cubic inch of space is a miracle'. Appreciation is a repeated theme, and there is thankfulness inscribed here that is tremendous in scope and vast in feeling, rooted in the traditions of the Iroquois and the Orthodox Synagogue as well as bubbling up in individuals. Each of us has been the beneficiary of 'tens of thousands / Of kindnesses' and to meditate on these is to be flooded with a calm and grateful delight.

It is far from easy, but these poems also remind us that the surest route to contentment is to live with both feet firmly planted, free of fret, in the present. A Sanskrit salutation to the dawn reminds us that:

> today well-spent makes every yesterday
> A dream of happiness
> And every tomorrow a vision of hope.

The soothing comfort of community and home, of kindnesses bestowed as well as received is not to be underestimated. In 'Trust', Lawrence asserts that the services and the tenderness we render to others will transfigure us:

> till we both of us
> are more glorious
> and more sunny.

As Emily Dickinson writes:

Preface

> If I can stop one heart from breaking,
> I shall not live in vain.

Who would not feel serene at the thought of adding to the world's store of goodness? This collection is map and compass, and in these pages are beautiful paths to peace, set down by people over hundreds of years for us to follow, at our own gentle pace. Turn the page, breathe deeply and take the first step.

MEDITATIONS

To Every Thing There Is a Season

To every thing there is a season,
and a time to every purpose under the heaven:
A time to be born, and a time to die;
A time to plant, and a time to pluck up that which is
    planted;
A time to kill, and a time to heal;
A time to break down, and a time to build up;
A time to weep, and a time to laugh;
A time to mourn, and a time to dance;
A time to cast away stones, and a time to gather
    stones together;
A time to embrace, and a time to refrain from
    embracing;
A time to get, and a time to lose;
A time to keep, and a time to cast away;
A time to rend, and a time to sew;
A time to keep silence, and a time to speak;
A time to love, and a time to hate;
A time of war, and a time of peace.

Book of Ecclesiastes

Invictus

Out of the night that covers me,
Black as the pit from pole to pole,
I thank whatever gods may be
For my unconquerable soul.

In the fell clutch of circumstance
I have not winced nor cried aloud.
Under the bludgeonings of chance
My head is bloody, but unbowed.

Beyond this place of wrath and tears
Looms but the Horror of the shade,
And yet the menace of the years
Finds and shall find me unafraid.

It matters not how strait the gate,
How charged with punishments the scroll,
I am the master of my fate,
I am the captain of my soul.

W. E. Henley (1849–1903)

Say Not the Struggle Nought Availeth

Say not the struggle nought availeth,
    The labour and the wounds are vain,
The enemy faints not, nor faileth,
    And as things have been they remain.

If hopes were dupes, fears may be liars;
    It may be, in yon smoke concealed,
Your comrades chase e'en now the fliers,
    And, but for you, possess the field.

For while the tired waves, vainly breaking,
    Seem here no painful inch to gain,
Far back through creeks and inlets making
    Comes silent, flooding in, the main,

And not by eastern windows only,
    When daylight comes, comes in the light,
In front the sun climbs slow, how slowly,
    But westward, look, the land is bright.

Arthur Hugh Clough (1819–1861)

If –

If you can keep your head when all about you
    Are losing theirs and blaming it on you,
If you can trust yourself when all men doubt you,
    But make allowance for their doubting too;
If you can wait and not be tired by waiting,
    Or being lied about, don't deal in lies,
Or being hated, don't give way to hating,
    And yet don't look too good, nor talk too wise:

If you can dream – and not make dreams your master;
    If you can think – and not make thoughts
        your aim;
If you can meet with Triumph and Disaster
    And treat those two impostors just the same;
If you can bear to hear the truth you've spoken
    Twisted by knaves to make a trap for fools,
Or watch the things you gave your life to, broken,
    And stoop and build 'em up with worn-out tools:

If you can make one heap of all your winnings
    And risk it on one turn of pitch-and-toss,
And lose, and start again at your beginnings
    And never breathe a word about your loss;
If you can force your heart and nerve and sinew
    To serve your turn long after they are gone,
And so hold on when there is nothing in you
    Except the Will which says to them: 'Hold on!'

If you can talk with crowds and keep your virtue,
    Or walk with Kings – nor lose the common
        touch,

If neither foes nor loving friends can hurt you,
    If all men count with you, but none too much;
If you can fill the unforgiving minute
    With sixty seconds' worth of distance run,
Yours is the Earth and everything that's in it,
    And – which is more – you'll be a Man, my son!

Rudyard Kipling (1865–1936)

Eternity

He who binds to himself a joy
Does the winged life destroy
He who kisses the joy as it flies
Lives in eternity's sunrise

William Blake (1757–1827)

from The Mask of Anarchy

Rise like Lions after slumber
In unvanquishable number,
Shake your chains to earth like dew
Which in sleep had fallen on you –
Ye are many – they are few.

Percy Bysshe Shelley (1792–1822)

from Auguries of Innocence

To see a World in a Grain of Sand
    And a Heaven in a Wild Flower,
Hold Infinity in the palm of your hand
    And Eternity in an hour.

William Blake (1757–1827)

Sonnet XXV

Let those who are in favour with their stars
Of public honour and proud titles boast,
Whilst I, whom fortune of such triumph bars,
Unlook'd-for joy in that I honour most.
Great princes' favourites their fair leaves spread
But as the marigold at the sun's eye,
And in themselves their pride lies buried,
For at a frown they in their glory die.
The painful warrior famoused for might,
After a thousand victories once foil'd
Is from the book of honour razed quite,
And all the rest forgot for which he toil'd.
    Then happy I, that love and am belov'd
    Where I may not remove nor be remov'd

William Shakespeare (1564–1616)

Going Down Hill on a Bicycle: A Boy's Song

With lifted feet, hands still,
I am poised, and down the hill
Dart, with heedful mind;
The air goes by in a wind.

Swifter and yet more swift,
Till the heart with a mighty lift
Makes the lungs laugh, the throat cry:–
'O bird, see; see, bird, I fly.

'Is this, is this your joy?
O bird, then I, though a boy,
For a golden moment share
Your feathery life in air!'

Say, heart, is there aught like this
In a world that is full of bliss?
'Tis more than skating, bound
Steel-shod to the level ground.

Speed slackens now, I float
Awhile in my airy boat;
Till, when the wheels scarce crawl,
My feet to the treadles fall.

Alas, that the longest hill
Must end in a vale; but still,
Who climbs with toil, wheresoe'er,
Shall find wings waiting there.

Henry Charles Beeching (1859–1919)

Leisure

What is this life if, full of care,
We have no time to stand and stare? –

No time to stand beneath the boughs,
And stare as long as sheep and cows:

No time to see, when woods we pass,
Where squirrels hide their nuts in grass:

No time to see, in broad daylight,
Streams full of stars, like skies at night:

No time to turn at Beauty's glance,
And watch her feet, how they can dance:

No time to wait till her mouth can
Enrich that smile her eyes began?

A poor life this if, full of care,
We have no time to stand and stare.

W. H. Davies (1871–1940)

NATURE

New Every Morning

Every day is a fresh beginning,
Listen my soul to the glad refrain.
   And, spite of old sorrows
         And older sinning,
         Troubles forecasted
         And possible pain,
Take heart with the day and begin again.

Susan Coolidge (1835–1905)

from Pippa Passes

The year's at the spring
And day's at the morn;
Morning's at seven;
The hillside's dew-pearled;
The lark's on the wing;
The snail's on the thorn:
God's in His heaven—
All's right with the world!

Robert Browning (1812–1889)

I Wandered Lonely as a Cloud

I wandered lonely as a cloud
That floats on high o'er vales and hills,
When all at once I saw a crowd,
A host, of golden daffodils;
Beside the lake, beneath the trees,
Fluttering and dancing in the breeze.

Continuous as the stars that shine
And twinkle on the milky way,
They stretched in never-ending line
Along the margin of a bay:
Ten thousand saw I at a glance,
Tossing their heads in sprightly dance.

The waves beside them danced; but they
Out-did the sparkling waves in glee:
A poet could not but be gay,
In such a jocund company:
I gazed—and gazed—but little thought
What wealth the show to me had brought:

For oft, when on my couch I lie
In vacant or in pensive mood,
They flash upon that inward eye
Which is the bliss of solitude;
And then my heart with pleasure fills,
And dances with the daffodils.

William Wordsworth (1770–1850)

A Greeting

Good morning, Life – and all
Things glad and beautiful.
My pockets nothing hold,
But he that owns the gold,
The Sun, is my great friend –
His spending has no end.

Hail to the morning sky,
Whose bright clouds measure high;
Hail to you birds whose throats
Would number leaves by notes;
Hail to you shady bowers,
And you green fields of flowers.

Hail to you women fair,
That make a show so rare
In cloth as white as milk –
Be't calico or silk:
Good morning, Life – and all
Things glad and beautiful.

W. H. Davies (1871–1940)

New Sights

I like to see a thing I know
Has not been seen before,
That's why I cut my apple through
To look into the core.

It's nice to think, though many an eye
Has seen the ruddy skin,
Mine is the very first to spy
The five brown pips within.

Anon.

My Heart Leaps Up When I Behold

My heart leaps up when I behold
           A rainbow in the sky:
So was it when my life began;
So is it now I am a man;
So be it when I shall grow old,
           Or let me die!
The Child is father of the Man;
And I could wish my days to be
Bound each to each by natural piety.

William Wordsworth (1770–1850)

'See yonder leafless trees against the sky'

See yonder leafless trees against the sky,
How they diffuse themselves into the air,
And ever subdividing separate,
Limbs into branches, branches into twigs,
As if they loved the element, & hasted
To dissipate their being into it.

Ralph Waldo Emerson (1803–1882)

Fragment 105(a)

    – O fair – O sweet!
As the sweet apple blooms high on the bough,
High as the highest, forgot of the gatherers:
    So thou: –
Yet not so: nor forgot of the gatherers;
High o'er their reach in the golden air,
    – O sweet – O fair!

Sappho (c. 630–570 BCE)
tr. F. T. Palgrave

A Fine Day

After all the rain, the sun
Shines on hill and grassy mead;
Fly into the garden, child,
You are very glad indeed.

For the days have been so dull,
Oh, so special dark and drear,
That you told me, 'Mr Sun
Has forgotten we live here.'

Dew upon the lily lawn,
Dew upon the garden beds;
Daintily from all the leaves
Pop the little primrose heads.

And the violets in the copse
With their parasols of green
Take a little peek at you;
They're the bluest you have seen.

On the lilac tree a bird
Singing first a little note,
Then a burst of happy song
Bubbles in his lifted throat.

O the sun, the comfy sun!
This the song that you must sing,
'Thank you for the birds, the flowers,
Thank you, sun, for everything.'

Katherine Mansfield (1888–1923)

There will come soft rains

There will come soft rains and the smell of the ground,
And swallows circling with their shimmering sound;

And frogs in the pools singing at night,
And wild plum trees in tremulous white;

Robins will wear their feathery fire,
Whistling their whims on a low fence-wire;

And not one will know of the war, not one
Will care at last when it is done.

Not one would mind, neither bird nor tree,
If mankind perished utterly;

And Spring herself, when she woke at dawn
Would scarcely know that we were gone.

Sara Teasdale (1884–1933)

Love Shall Stay

The rose is dead, and the honey-bee
Forsakes the empty flower,
And summer has sailed across the sea,
Away from a leafless bower.

And the singing birds, to the siren south,
Have followed the sunbeam's track,
And never a word in his frozen mouth
Has the year to hail them back.

And rosy Love, with his eyes of dawn,
And his cheek of dimpling laughter –
How shall he live where the skies are wan?
Ah me! Will he up, and after?

The swallow may go, and the sun depart,
And the rose's bloom decay,
But I'll make a summer within my heart,
And Love, sweet Love, shall stay!

Margaret Armour (1860–1943)

The Happy Child

I saw this day sweet flowers grow thick –
But not one like the child did pick.

I heard the pack-hounds in green park –
But no dog like the child heard bark.

I heard this day bird after bird –
But not one like the child has heard.

A hundred butterflies saw I –
But not one like the child saw fly.

I saw horses roll in grass –
But no horse like the child saw pass.

My world this day has lovely been –
But not like what the child has seen.

W. H. Davies (1871–1940)

The Lake Isle of Innisfree

I will arise and go now, and go to Innisfree,
And a small cabin build there, of clay and wattles
    made:
Nine bean-rows will I have there, a hive for the
    honey-bee,
And live alone in the bee-loud glade.

And I shall have some peace there, for peace comes
    dropping slow,
Dropping from the veils of the morning to where the
    cricket sings;
There midnight's all a glimmer, and noon a purple
    glow,
And evening full of the linnet's wings.

I will arise and go now, for always night and day
I hear lake water lapping with low sounds by the shore;
While I stand on the roadway, or on the pavements
    grey,
I hear it in the deep heart's core.

W. B. Yeats (1865–1939)

Sowing

It was a perfect day
For sowing; just
As sweet and dry was the ground
As tobacco-dust.

I tasted deep the hour
Between the far
Owl's chuckling first soft cry
And the first star.

A long stretched hour it was;
Nothing undone
Remained; the early seeds
All safely sown.

And now, hark at the rain,
Windless and light,
Half a kiss, half a tear,
Saying good-night.

Edward Thomas (1878–1917)

Gratitude to the Unknown Instructors

What they undertook to do
They brought to pass;
All things hang like a drop of dew
Upon a blade of grass.

W. B. Yeats (1865–1939)

from A Midsummer Night's Dream

I know a bank where the wild thyme blows,
Where oxlips and the nodding violet grows,
Quite over-canopied with luscious woodbine,
With sweet musk-roses and with eglantine:
There sleeps Titania sometime of the night,
Lulled in these flowers with dances and delight.

William Shakespeare (1564–1616)

Pied Beauty

Glory be to God for dappled things –
    For skies of couple-colour as a brinded cow;
        For rose-moles all in stipple upon trout that
            swim;
Fresh-firecoal chestnut-falls; finches' wings;
      Landscape plotted and pieced – fold, fallow,
         and plough;
      And áll trádes, their gear and tackle and trim.

All things counter, original, spare, strange;
    Whatever is fickle, freckled (who knows how?)
        With swift, slow; sweet, sour; adazzle, dim;
He fathers-forth whose beauty is past change:
        Praise him.

Gerard Manley Hopkins (1844–1889)

Green

The dawn was apple-green,
The sky was green wine held up in the sun,
The moon was a golden petal between.

She opened her eyes, and green
They shone, clear like flowers undone
For the first time, now for the first time seen.

D. H. Lawrence (1885–1930)

Tall Nettles

Tall nettles cover up, as they have done
    These many springs, the rusty harrow, the plough
Long worn out, and the roller made of stone;
    Only the elm butt tops the nettles now.

This corner of the farmyard I like most:
    As well as any bloom upon a flower
I like the dust on the nettles, never lost
    Except to prove the sweetness of a shower.

Edward Thomas (1878–1917)

My Voysey Wall-Paper

I have two gardens for my ease,
Where skies are warm and flowers please;
With skilful mastery each designed
Is fair and perfect of its kind.
In one the tulips every year
Flame April out and disappear;
And roses red that garland June
Are worn but for a summer's noon.
It is a garden, flower and leaf,
Where lovely things are very brief.

Upon a wall my other grows,
And changes not for heat or snows.
Its tulips do not flaunt and die,
But, dreaming, watch the spring go by.
In pensive grey, like musing nuns,
They hold no commerce with the suns.
There leaves in order are outspread
Which ruffling winds shall never shed.
The roses are the magic blue
That in the faery gardens grew,
Not fashioned for themselves alone,
But for the common beauty grown.

They shall not wax, they shall not wane,
They shall not flush to fleet again,
But quaintly, in their quiet place,

Shall charm me with unaltered grace,
And fresh for ever, flower and shoot,
Shall spring from their eternal root.

Margaret Armour (1860–1943)

Flowers and Trees

Boon nature scattered, free and wild,
Each plant or flower, the mountain's child.
Here eglantine embalmed the air,
Hawthorn and hazel mingled there;
The primrose pale, and violet flower,
Found in such cliff a narrow bower;
Fox-glove and night-shade, side by side,
Emblems of punishment and pride,
Grouped their dark hues with every stain
The weather-beaten crags retain.
With boughs that quaked at every breath,
Grey birch and aspen wept beneath;
Aloft, the ash and warrior oak
Cast anchor in the rifted rock;
And, higher yet, the pine-tree hung
His shattered trunk, and frequent flung,
Where seemed the cliffs to meet on high,
His boughs athwart the narrowed sky.
Highest of all, where white peaks glanced,
Where glistening streamers waved and danced.
The wanderer's eye could barely view
The summer heaven's delicious blue;
So wonderous wild, the whole might seem
The scenery of a fairy dream.

Sir Walter Scott (1771–1832)

To the Fox Fern

Haunter of woods, lone wilds and solitudes
Where none but feet of birds and things as wild
Doth print a foot track near, where summer's light
Buried in boughs forgets its glare and round thy crimpèd
    leaves
Faints in a quiet dimness fit for musings
And melancholy moods, with here and there
A golden thread of sunshine stealing through
The evening shadowy leaves that seem to creep
Like leisure in the shade.

John Clare (1793–1864)

To Autumn

Season of mists and mellow fruitfulness,
    Close bosom-friend of the maturing sun;
Conspiring with him how to load and bless
    With fruit the vines that round the thatch-eaves
        run;
To bend with apples the mossed cottage-trees,
    And fill all fruit with ripeness to the core;
        To swell the gourd, and plump the hazel shells
    With a sweet kernel; to set budding more,
And still more, later flowers for the bees,
Until they think warm days will never cease,
    For Summer has o'er-brimmed their clammy cells.

Who hath not seen thee oft amid thy store?
    Sometimes whoever seeks abroad may find
Thee sitting careless on a granary floor,
    Thy hair soft-lifted by the winnowing wind;
Or on a half-reaped furrow sound asleep,
    Drowsed with the fume of poppies, while thy hook
        Spares the next swath and all its twinèd
           flowers:
    And sometimes like a gleaner thou dost keep
Steady thy laden head across a brook;
Or by a cider-press, with patient look,
    Thou watchest the last oozings, hours by hours.

Where are the songs of Spring? Ay, where are they?
    Think not of them, thou hast thy music too –
While barrèd clouds bloom the soft-dying day,
    And touch the stubble-plains with rosy hue;

Then in a wailful choir the small gnats mourn
 Among the river sallows, borne aloft
  Or sinking as the light wind lives or dies;
 And full-grown lambs loud bleat from hilly bourn;
Hedge-crickets sing; and now with treble soft
The red-breast whistles from a garden-croft;
 And gathering swallows twitter in the skies.

John Keats (1795–1821)

The Way Through the Woods

They shut the road through the woods
    Seventy years ago.
Weather and rain have undone it again,
    And now you would never know
There was once a road through the woods
    Before they planted the trees.
It is underneath the coppice and heath,
    And the thin anemones.
Only the keeper sees
    That, where the ring-dove broods,
And the badgers roll at ease,
    There was once a road through the woods.

Yet, if you enter the woods
    Of a summer evening late,
When the night-air cools on the trout-ringed pools
    Where the otter whistles his mate,
(They fear not men in the woods,
    Because they see so few)
You will hear the beat of a horse's feet
    And the swish of a skirt in the dew,
    Steadily cantering through
The misty solitudes,
    As though they perfectly knew
The old lost road through the woods . . .
    But there is no road through the woods.

Rudyard Kipling (1865–1936)

'It is a beauteous evening, calm and free'

It is a beauteous evening, calm and free,
The holy time is quiet as a Nun
Breathless with adoration; the broad sun
Is sinking down in its tranquillity;
The gentleness of heaven broods o'er the Sea:
Listen! the mighty Being is awake,
And doth with his eternal motion make
A sound like thunder – everlastingly.
Dear Child! dear Girl! that walkest with me here,
If thou appear untouched by solemn thought,
Thy nature is not therefore less divine:
Thou liest in Abraham's bosom all the year;
And worshipp'st at the Temple's inner shrine,
God being with thee when we know it not.

William Wordsworth (1770–1850)

FRIENDSHIP AND GRATITUDE

Friendship

Oh, the comfort –
the inexpressible comfort of feeling *safe* with a person –
having neither to weigh thoughts nor measure words,
but pouring them all right out,
just as they are,
chaff and grain together;
certain that a faithful hand will take and sift them,
keep what is worth keeping,
and then with the breath of kindness blow the rest away.

Dinah Maria Craik (1826–1887)

The Earth-Child in the Grass

In the very early morning
Long before Dawn time
I lay down in the paddock
And listened to the cold song of the grass.
Between my fingers the green blades,
And the green blades pressed against my body.
'Who is she leaning so heavily upon me?'
Sang the grass.
'Why does she weep on my bosom,
Mingling her tears with the tears of my mystic lover?
Foolish little earth child!
It is not yet time.
One day I shall open my bosom
And you shall slip in – but not weeping.
Then in the early morning
Long before Dawn time
Your lover will lie in the paddock.
Between his fingers the green blades
And the green blades pressed against his body . . .
My song shall not sound cold to him
In my deep wave he will find the wave of your hair
In my strong sweet perfume, the perfume of your kisses.
Long and long he will lie there . . .
Laughing – not weeping.'

Katherine Mansfield (1888–1923)

The Consolation

Though bleak these woods, and damp the ground
With fallen leaves so thickly strown,
And cold the wind that wanders round
With wild and melancholy moan;

There *is* a friendly roof, I know,
Might shield me from the wintry blast;
There is a fire, whose ruddy glow
Will cheer me for my wanderings past.

And so, though still, where'er I go,
Cold stranger-glances meet my eye;
Though, when my spirit sinks in woe,
Unheeded swells the unbidden sigh;

Though solitude, endured too long,
Bids youthful joys too soon decay,
Makes mirth a stranger to my tongue,
And overclouds my noon of day;

When kindly thoughts, that would have way,
Flow back discouraged to my breast; –
I know there *is*, though far away,
A home where heart and soul may rest.

Warm hands are there, that, clasped in mine,
The warmer heart will not belie;
While mirth, and truth, and friendship shine
In smiling lip and earnest eye.

The ice that gathers round my heart
May there be thawed; and sweetly, then,
The joys of youth, that now depart,
Will come to cheer my soul again.

Though far I roam, that thought shall be
My hope, my comfort, everywhere;
While such a home remains to me,
My heart shall never know despair!

Anne Brontë (1820–1849)

Beauty

What does it mean? Tired, angry, and ill at ease,
No man, woman, or child alive could please
Me now. And yet I almost dare to laugh
Because I sit and frame an epitaph –
'Here lies all that no one loved of him
And that loved no one.' Then in a trice that whim
Has wearied. But, though I am like a river
At fall of evening when it seems that never
Has the sun lighted it or warmed it, while
Cross breezes cut the surface to a file,
This heart, some fraction of me, happily
Floats through a window even now to a tree
Down in the misting, dim-lit, quiet vale;
Not like a pewit that returns to wail
For something it has lost, but like a dove
That slants unanswering to its home and love.
There I find my rest, and through the dusk air
Flies what yet lives in me. Beauty is there.

Edward Thomas (1878-1917)

Your Task

Your task is not to seek for love,
but merely to seek and find all the barriers within
    yourself
that you have built against it.

Rumi (1207–1273) tr. Anon.

If I Can Stop One Heart from Breaking

If I can stop one heart from breaking,
    I shall not live in vain;
If I can ease one life the aching,
    Or cool one pain,
Or help one lonely person
    Into happiness again
I shall not live in vain.

Emily Dickinson (1830–1886)

Man is Dear to Man

Man is dear to man: the poorest poor
Long for some moments in a weary life
When they can know and feel that they have been
Themselves the fathers and the givers-out
Of some small blessings; have been kind to such
As needed kindness, for the single cause
That we have all of us one common heart.

William Wordsworth (1770–1850)

Forbearance

Hast thou named all the birds without a gun?
Loved the wood-rose, and left it on its stalk?
At rich men's tables eaten bread and pulse?
Unarmed, faced danger with a heart of trust?
And loved so well a high behavior,
In man or maid, that thou from speech refrained,
Nobility more nobly to repay?
O, be my friend, and teach me to be thine!

Ralph Waldo Emerson (1803–1882)

Trust

Oh we've got to trust
one another again
in some essentials.

Not the narrow little
bargaining trust
that says: I'm for you
if you'll be for me. –

But a bigger trust,
a trust of the sun
that does not bother
about moth and rust,
and we see it shining
in one another.

Oh don't you trust me,
don't burden me
with your life and affairs; don't
thrust me
into your cares.

But I think you may trust
the sun in me
that glows with just
as much glow as you see
in me, and no more.

But if it warms
your heart's quick core

why then trust it, it forms
one faithfulness more.

And be, oh be
a sun to me,
not a weary, insistent
personality

but a sun that shines
and goes dark, but shines
again and entwines
with the sunshine in me

till we both of us
are more glorious
and more sunny.

D. H. Lawrence (1885–1930)

Sonnet: I Thank You

I thank you, kind and best beloved friend,
With the same thanks one murmurs to a sister,
When, for some gentle favor, he hath kissed her,
Less for the gifts than for the love you send,
Less for the flowers, than what the flowers convey;
If I, indeed, divine their meaning truly,
And not unto myself ascribe, unduly,
Things which you neither meant nor wished to say,
Oh! tell me, is the hope then all misplaced?
And am I flattered by my own affection?
But in your beauteous gift, methought I traced
Something above a short-lived predilection,
And which, for that I know no dearer name,
I designate as love, without love's flame.

Henry Timrod (1828–1867)

Gratefulnesse

Thou that hast giv'n so much to me,
Give one thing more, a gratefull heart.
See how thy beggar works on thee
                              By art.

He makes thy gifts occasion more,
And sayes, If he in this be crost,
All thou hast giv'n him heretofore
                              Is lost.

But thou didst reckon, when at first
Thy word our hearts and hands did crave,
What it would come to at the worst
                              To save.

Perpetuall knockings at thy doore,
Tears sullying thy transparent rooms,
Gift upon gift, much would have more,
                              And comes.

This notwithstanding, thou wentst on,
And didst allow us all our noise:
Nay, thou hast made a sigh and grone
                              Thy joyes.

Not that thou hast not still above
Much better tunes, then grones can make;
But that these countrey-aires thy love
                              Did take.

Wherefore I crie, and crie again;
And in no quiet canst thou be,
Till I a thankfull heart obtain

> Of thee:

Not thankfull, when it pleaseth me;
As if thy blessings had spare dayes:
But such a heart, whose pulse may be

> Thy praise.

George Herbert (1593–1633)

Friendship

Like a quetzal plume, a fragrant flower,
friendship sparkles:
like heron plumes, it weaves itself into finery.
Our song is a bird calling out like a jingle:
how beautiful you make it sound!
Here, among flowers that enclose us,
among flowery boughs you are singing.

Aztec, Traditional

Sonnet XXX

When to the sessions of sweet silent thought
I summon up remembrance of things past,
I sigh the lack of many a thing I sought,
And with old woes new wail my dear time's waste:
Then can I drown an eye, unused to flow,
For precious friends hid in death's dateless night,
And weep afresh love's long since cancelled woe,
And moan the expense of many a vanished sight:
Then can I grieve at grievances foregone,
And heavily from woe to woe tell o'er
The sad account of fore-bemoanèd moan,
Which I new pay as if not paid before.
    But if the while I think on thee, dear friend,
    All losses are restored and sorrows end.

William Shakespeare (1564–1616)

When I have fears

When I have fears that I may cease to be
    Before my pen has gleaned my teeming brain,
Before high-pilèd books, in charactery,
    Hold like rich garners the full ripened grain;
When I behold, upon the night's starred face,
    Huge cloudy symbols of a high romance,
And think that I may never live to trace
    Their shadows with the magic hand of chance;
And when I feel, fair creature of an hour,
    That I shall never look upon thee more,
Never have relish in the faery power
    Of unreflecting love – then on the shore
Of the wide world I stand alone, and think
    Till love and fame to nothingness do sink.

John Keats (1795–1821)

Consolation

Though he, that ever kind and true,
Kept stoutly step by step with you,
Your whole long gusty lifetime through,
    Be gone awhile before,
Be now a moment gone before,
Yet, doubt not, soon the seasons shall restore
    Your friend to you.

He has but turned a corner – still
He pushes on with right good will,
Through mire and marsh, by heugh and hill,
    That self-same arduous way –
That self-same upland, hopeful way
That you and he through many a doubtful day
    Attempted still.

He is not dead, this friend – not dead,
But in the path we mortals tread
Got some few trifling steps ahead
    And nearer to the end;
So that you too, once past the bend,
Shall meet again, as face to face, this friend
    You fancy dead.

Push gaily on, strong heart! The while
You travel forward mile by mile,
He loiters with a backward smile
    Till you can overtake,

And strains his eyes to search his wake,
Or whistling, as he sees you through the brake,
    Waits on a stile.

                Robert Louis Stevenson (1850–1894)

PRAYERS AND BLESSINGS

'All shall be well'

All shall be well
and all shall be well
and all manner of thing
shall be well.

Dame Julian of Norwich (1343–1416)

'Now may every living thing'

Now may every living thing, young or old, weak or strong, living near or far, known or unknown, living or departed or yet unborn, may every living thing be full of bliss.

The Buddha (c. 5th–4th century BCE)

God's Grandeur

The world is charged with the grandeur of God.
    It will flame out, like shining from shook foil;
    It gathers to a greatness, like the ooze of oil
Crushed. Why do men then now not reck his rod?
Generations have trod, have trod, have trod;
    And all is seared with trade; bleared, smeared
        with toil;
    And wears man's smudge and shares man's smell:
        the soil
Is bare now, nor can foot feel, being shod.

And for all this, nature is never spent;
    There lives the dearest freshness deep down things;
And though the last lights off the black West went
    Oh, morning, at the brown brink eastward, springs –
Because the Holy Ghost over the bent
    World broods with warm breast and with ah!
        bright wings.

Gerard Manley Hopkins (1844–1889)

Pax

All that matters is to be at one with the living God
to be a creature in the house of the God of Life.

Like a cat asleep on a chair
at peace, in peace
and at one with the master of the house, with the
   mistress,
at home, at home in the house of the living,
sleeping on the hearth, and yawning before the fire.

Sleeping on the hearth of the living world
yawning at home before the fire of life
feeling the presence of the living God
like a great reassurance
a deep calm in the heart
a presence
as of a master sitting at the board
in his own and greater being,
in the house of life.

D. H. Lawrence (1885–1930)

Desiderata

'Go placidly amid the noise and the haste, and remember what peace there may be in silence. As far as possible without surrender be on good terms with all persons. Speak your truth quietly and clearly; and listen to others, even the dull and ignorant; they too have their story. Avoid loud and aggressive persons, they are vexatious to the spirit. If you compare yourself with others you may become vain and bitter; for always there will be greater and lesser persons than yourself. Enjoy your achievements as well as your plans. Keep interested in your own career, however humble; it is a real possession in the changing fortunes of time. Exercise caution in your business affairs; for the world is full of trickery. But let this not blind you to what virtue there is; many persons strive for high ideals; and everywhere life is full of heroism. Be yourself. Especially do not feign affection. Neither be cynical about love; for in the face of all aridity and disenchantment it is as perennial as the grass. Take kindly the counsel of the years, gracefully surrendering the things of youth. Nurture strength of spirit to shield you in sudden misfortune. But do not distress yourself with imaginings. Many fears are born of fatigue and loneliness. Beyond a wholesome discipline, be gentle with yourself. You are a child of the universe no less than the trees and the stars; you have a right to be here. And whether or not it is clear to you, no doubt the universe is unfolding as it should. Therefore be at peace with God, whatever you conceive Him to be. And whatever your labors and aspirations, in the noisy confusion of life keep peace with your soul. With all its sham, drudgery and broken dreams, it is still a beautiful world. Be cheerful. Strive to be happy.'

Max Ehrmann (1872–1945)

Bani Adam

Human beings are members of a whole,
In creation of one essence and soul.
If one member is afflicted with pain,
Other members uneasy will remain.
If you've no sympathy for human pain,
The name of human you cannot retain!

Saadi Shirazi (1210–1291)

On Children

Your children are not your children.
They are the sons and daughters of Life's longing for
    itself.
They come through you but not from you,
And though they are with you, yet they belong not
    to you.

You may give them your love but not your thoughts,
For they have their own thoughts.
You may house their bodies but not their souls,
For their souls dwell in the house of tomorrow,
Which you cannot visit, not even in your dreams.
You may strive to be like them,
But seek not to make them like you.
For life goes not backward nor tarries with yesterday.

You are the bows from which your children
As living arrows are sent forth.
The archer sees the mark upon the path of the infinite,
And He bends you with His might
That His arrows may go swift and far.
Let your bending in the archer's hand be for gladness;
For even as He loves the arrow that flies,
So He loves also the bow that is stable.

Khalil Gibran (1883–1931)

A Sanskrit Salutation To The Dawn

Look to this day for it is life, the very life of life.
In its brief course lie all the verities and realities
Of our existence.
The bliss of growth, the splendor of beauty,
For yesterday is but a dream
And tomorrow is only a vision,
But today well-spent makes every yesterday
A dream of happiness
And every tomorrow a vision of hope.
Look well therefore to this day.
Such is the salutation to the dawn.

Anon.

The Song of Blessing

Not to serve the foolish, but to serve the wise,
To honour those worthy of honour – this is the
    highest blessing.

Much insight and education, self-control and pleasant
    speech,
And whatever word be well-spoken – this is the
    highest blessing.

Service to mother and father, the company of wife
    and child,
And peaceful pursuits – this is the highest blessing.

Almsgiving and righteousness, the company of
    kinsfolk,
Blameless works – this is the highest blessing.

To dwell in a pleasant land, with right desire in the
    heart,
To bear remembrance of good deeds – this is the
    highest blessing.

Reverence and humility, cheerfulness and gratitude,
    listening in due season to the Dhamma – this is
    the highest blessing.

Self-control and virtue, vision of the Noble Truths,
And winning to Nirvana – this is the highest blessing.

Beneath the stroke of life's changes, the mind that
    does not shake

But abides without grief or passion – this is the
    highest blessing.

On every side invincible are they who do thus,
They come to salvation – theirs is the highest blessing.

from The Sutta Nipāta *(Pre-100 BC)*

from The Vedas

May there be peace in the higher regions; may there be peace in the firmament; may there be peace on earth. May the waters flow peacefully; may the herbs and plants grow peacefully; may all the divine powers bring unto us peace. The supreme Lord is peace. May we all be in peace, peace, and only peace; and may that peace come unto each of us.

Shanti [Peace] – *Shanti– Shanti!*

Anon.

'Lord, make me an instrument of Thy peace'

Lord, make me an instrument of Thy peace.
Where there is hatred, let me sow love;
Where there is injury, pardon;
Where there is doubt, faith;
When there is despair, hope;
Where there is darkness, light;
When there is sadness, joy.

O Divine Master, grant that
I may not so much seek
To be consoled, as to console;
Not so much to be understood as
To understand; not so much to be
Loved as to love:
For it is in giving that we receive;
It is in pardoning, that we are pardoned;
It is in dying, that we awaken to eternal life.

St Francis of Assisi (1182–1226)

God Be In My Head

God be in my head
And in my understanding;
God be in myne eyes,
And in my looking;
God be in my mouth,
And in my speaking;
God be in my heart,
And in my thynking;
God be at my end,
And at my departing.

Sarum Missal (11th century)

The Thanksgivings

We who are here present thank the Great Spirit that
    we are here to praise Him.

We thank Him that He has created men and women,
    and ordered that these beings shall always be
    living to multiply the earth.

We thank Him for making the earth and giving
    these beings its products to live on.

We thank Him for the water that comes out of
    the earth and runs for our lands.

We thank Him for all the animals on the earth.

We thank Him for certain timbers that grow and
    have fluids coming from them for us all.

We thank Him for the branches of the trees that
    grow shadows for our shelter.

We thank Him for the beings that come from the
    west, the thunder and lightning that water the earth.

We thank Him for the light which we call our oldest
    brother, the sun that works for our good.

We thank Him for all the fruits that grow on the
    trees and vines.

We thank Him for his goodness in making the forests,
    and thank all its trees.

We thank Him for the darkness that gives us rest, and
    for the kind Being of the darkness that gives us
    light, the moon.

We thank Him for the bright spots in the skies that
    give us signs, the stars.

We give Him thanks for our supporters, who had
    charge of our harvests.

We give thanks that the voice of the Great Spirit can
    still be heard through the words of Ga-ne-o-di-o.
We thank the Great Spirit that we have the privilege
    of this pleasant occasion.
We give thanks for the persons who can sing the
    Great Spirit's music, and hope they will be
    privileged to continue in his faith.
We thank the Great Spirit for all the persons who
    perform the ceremonies on this occasion.

Iroquois, Traditional tr. Harriet Maxwell
Converse (1836–1903)

The Iroquois Prayer

We return thanks to our mother, the earth, which
    sustains us.
We return thanks to the rivers and streams, which
    supply us with water.
We return thanks to all herbs, which furnish
    medicines for the cure of our diseases.
We return thanks to the corn, and to her sisters, the
    beans and squash, which give us life.
We return thanks to the bushes and trees, which
    provide us with fruit.
We return thanks to the wind which, moving the air,
    has banished diseases.
We return thanks to the moon and the stars, which
    have given us their light when the sun was gone.
We return thanks to our grandfather He-no, who has
    given to us his rain.
We return thanks to the sun, that he has looked upon
    the earth with a beneficent eye.
Lastly, we return thanks to the Great Spirit, in whom
    is embodied all goodness, and who directs all
        things
    for the good of his children.

Iroquois, Traditional

Jewish Prayer

Though our mouths were full of song as the sea,
Our tongues of exultation as the fullness of its waves,
And our lips of praise as the plains of the firmament:

Though our eyes gave light as the sun and moon:
Though our hands were outspread as the eagles
    of heaven,
And our feet were swift as hinds,

Yet should we be unable to thank Thee,
O Lord our God and God of our fathers,
And to bless Thy Name for even one of the countless
    thousands
And tens of thousands
Of kindnesses which Thou hast done by our fathers
    and by us.

Service of the Orthodox Synagogue for
the Festival of Tabernacles

A Prayer for Travellers

May the road rise up to meet you.
May the wind be always at your back.
May the sun shine warm upon your face;
The rains fall soft upon your fields.
And until we meet again,
May God hold you in the palm of His hand.

Anon.

Gaelic Blessing

from Carmina Gadelica

Beannachd Dhè a bhith agaibh,
'S guma math a dh'èireas dhuibh;
Beannachd Chriosda a bhith agaibh,
'S guma math a chuirear ruibh;
Beannachd Spioraid a bhith agaibh,
'S guma math a chuireas sibh seachad bhur saoghal,
Gach latha dh'èireas sibh a suas,
Gath oidhche laigheas sibh a slos.

God's blessing be yours,
and well may it befall you;
Christ's blessing be yours,
And well be you entreated;
Spirit's blessing be yours,
And well spend you your lives,
Each day that you rise up,
Each night that you lie down.

Anon. tr. Alexander Carmichael (1832–1912)

from His Pilgrimage

Give me my scallop-shell of quiet,
My staff of faith to walk upon,
My scrip of joy, immortal diet,
My bottle of salvation,
My gown of Glory, hope's true gage;
And thus I'll take my pilgrimage.

Sir Walter Raleigh (c. 1554–1618)

Utitia'q's Song

Aja, I am joyful; this is good!
Aja, there is nothing but ice around me, that is good!
Aja, I am joyful; this is good!
My country is nothing but slush, that is good!
Aja, I am joyful; this is good!
Aja, when, indeed, will this end? this is good!
I am tired of watching and waking, this is good!

Inuit, Traditional tr. Franz Boaz (1858–1942)

Miracles

Why, who makes much of a miracle?
As to me I know of nothing else but miracles,
Whether I walk the streets of Manhattan,
Or dart my sight over the roofs of houses toward
   the sky,
Or wade with naked feet along the beach just in the
   edge of the water,
Or stand under trees in the woods,
Or talk by day with any one I love, or sleep in the bed
   at night with any one I love,
Or sit at table at dinner with the rest,
Or look at strangers opposite me riding in the car,
Or watch honey-bees busy around the hive of a
   summer forenoon,
Or animals feeding in the fields,
Or birds, or the wonderfulness of insects in the air,
Or the wonderfulness of the sundown, or of stars
   shining so quiet and bright,
Or the exquisite delicate thin curve of the new moon
   in spring;
These with the rest, one and all, are to me miracles,
The whole referring, yet each distinct and in its place.
To me every hour of the light and dark is a miracle,
Every cubic inch of space is a miracle,
Every square yard of the surface of the earth is spread
   with the same,
Every foot of the interior swarms with the same.
To me the sea is a continual miracle,

The fishes that swim – the rocks – the motion of the
    waves – the ships with men in them,
What stranger miracles are there?

Walt Whitman (1819–1892)

From The Brewing Of Soma

Dear Lord and Father of mankind,
    Forgive our foolish ways!
Reclothe us in our rightful mind,
In purer lives thy service find,
    In deeper reverence, praise.

In simple trust like theirs who heard
    Beside the Syrian sea
The gracious calling of the Lord,
Let us, like them, without a word,
    Rise up and follow thee.

O Sabbath rest by Galilee!
    O calm of hills above,
Where Jesus knelt to share with thee
The silence of eternity
    Interpreted by love!

With that deep hush subduing all
    Our words and works that drown
The tender whisper of thy call,
As noiseless let thy blessing fall
    As fell thy manna down.

Drop thy still dews of quietness,
    Till all our strivings cease;
Take from our souls the strain and stress,
And let our ordered lives confess
    The beauty of thy peace.

Breathe through the heats of our desire
        Thy coolness and thy balm;
Let sense be dumb, let flesh retire;
Speak through the earthquake, wind, and fire,
        O still, small voice of calm!

John Greenleaf Whittier (1807–1892)

Love is . . .

1 CORINTHIANS 13 (4–13)

Love is patient, love is kind. It does not envy, it does not boast, it is not proud. It does not dishonour others, it is not self-seeking, it is not easily angered, it keeps no record of wrongs. Love does not delight in evil but rejoices with the truth. It always protects, always trusts, always hopes, always perseveres.

Love never fails. But where there are prophecies, they will cease; where there are tongues, they will be stilled; where there is knowledge, it will pass away. For we know in part and we prophesy in part, but when completeness comes, what is in part disappears. When I was a child, I talked like a child, I thought like a child, I reasoned like a child. When I became a man, I put the ways of childhood behind me. For now we see only a reflection as in a mirror; then we shall see face to face. Now I know in part; then I shall know fully, even as I am fully known. And now these three remain: faith, hope and love. But the greatest of these is love.

Corinthians

The Song of a Man Who Has Come Through

Not I, not I, but the wind that blows through me!
A fine wind is blowing the new direction of Time.
If only I let it bear me, carry me, if only it carry me!
If only I am sensitive, subtle, oh, delicate, a winged
     gift!
If only, most lovely of all, I yield myself and am
     borrowed
By the fine, fine wind that takes its course through the
     chaos of the world
Like a fine, and exquisite chisel, a wedge-blade
     inserted;
If only I am keen and hard like the sheer tip of a wedge
Driven by invisible blows
The rock will split, we shall come at the wonder, we
     shall find the Hesperides
Oh, for the wonder that bubbles into my soul,
I would be a good fountain, a good well-head,
Would blur no whisper, spoil no expression.

What is the knocking?
What is the knocking at the door in the night?
It's somebody wants to do us harm.

No, no, it is the three strange angels.
Admit them, admit them.

D. H. Lawrence (1885–1930)

I Asked for Strength

I asked for strength that I might achieve;
I was made weak that I might learn humbly to obey.

I asked for health that I might do greater things;
I was given infirmity that I might do better things.

I asked for riches that I might be happy;
I was given poverty that I might be wise.

I asked for power that I might have the praise of men;
I was given weakness that I might feel the need of God.

I asked for all things that I might enjoy life;
I was given life that I might enjoy all things.

I got nothing that I had asked for,
but everything that I had hoped for.

Almost despite myself my unspoken prayers were
    answered;
I am, among all men, most richly blessed.

Prayer of an Unknown Confederate Soldier

Two Petitions

From the unreal lead me to the real.
From darkness lead me to light.
From death lead me to immortality.

The Upanishads (800 BC)

Ending Blessing

May it be beautiful before me.
May it be beautiful behind me.
May it be beautiful below me.
May it be beautiful above me.
May it be beautiful all around me.
In beauty it is finished.
In beauty it is finished.
Happily I go forth.

A Navajo Chant, Native American

Native American Prayer

When I am dead
Cry for me a little
Think of me sometimes
But not too much

Think of me now and again
As I was in life
At some moments it's pleasant to recall
But not for long

Leave me in peace
And I shall leave you in peace
And while you live
Let your thoughts be with the living

Anon.

Epitaph

God give me work
Till my life shall end
And life
Till my work is done.

Winifred Holtby (1898–1935)

SKY AND SEA

High Flight (An Airman's Ecstasy)

Oh, I have slipped the surly bonds of earth
And danced the skies on laughter-silvered wings;
Sunward I've climbed and joined the tumbling mirth
Of sun-split clouds – and done a hundred things
You have not dreamed of; wheeled and soared and
    swung
High in the sun-lit silence. Hovering there
I've chased the shouting wind along, and flung
My eager craft through footless halls of air;
Up, up the long, delirious, burning blue
I've topped the wind-swept heights with easy grace,
Where never lark nor even eagle flew;
And while, with silent lifting mind I've trod
The high untrespassed sanctity of space,
Put out my hand, and touched the face of God.

John Gillespie Magee (1922–1941)

Escape at Bedtime

The lights from the parlour and kitchen shone out
    Through the blinds and the windows and bars;
And high overhead and all moving about,
    There were thousands of millions of stars.

There ne'er were such thousands of leaves on a tree,
    Nor of people in church or the Park,
As the crowds of the stars that looked down upon me,
    And that glittered and winked in the dark.

The Dog, and the Plough, and the Hunter, and all,
    And the star of the sailor, and Mars,
These shone in the sky, and the pail by the wall
    Would be half full of water and stars.

They saw me at last, and they chased me with cries,
    And they soon had me packed into bed;
But the glory kept shining and bright in my eyes,
    And the stars going round in my head.

Robert Louis Stevenson (1850–1894)

Bright Star

Bright star, would I were steadfast as thou art –
Not in lone splendour hung aloft the night
And watching, with eternal lids apart,
Like nature's patient, sleepless Eremite,
The moving waters at their priest-like task
Of pure ablution round earth's human shores,
Or gazing on the new soft-fallen mask
Of snow upon the mountains and the moors –
No – yet still steadfast, still unchangeable,
Pillowed upon my fair love's ripening breast,
To feel for ever its soft fall and swell,
Awake for ever in a sweet unrest,
Still, still to hear her tender-taken breath,
And so live ever – or else swoon to death.

John Keats (1795–1821)

Ode

The spacious firmament on high,
With all the blue ethereal sky,
And spangled heav'ns, a shining frame,
Their great original proclaim:
Th' unwearied sun, from day to day,
Does his Creator's power display,
And publishes to every land
The work of an almighty hand.

Soon as the evening shades prevail,
The moon takes up the wondrous tale,
And nightly to the list'ning earth
Repeats the story of her birth:
Whilst all the stars that round her burn,
And all the planets in their turn,
Confirm the tidings as they roll,
And spread the truth from pole to pole.

What though, in solemn silence, all
Move round the dark terrestrial ball?
What though nor real voice nor sound
Amid their radiant orbs be found?
In reason's ear they all rejoice,
And utter forth a glorious voice,
For ever singing, as they shine,
'The hand that made us is divine.

Joseph Addison (1672–1719)

108

February Twilight

I stood beside a hill
    Smooth with new-laid snow,
A single star looked out
    From the cold evening glow.

There was no other creature
    That saw what I could see –
I stood and watched the evening star
    As long as it watched me.

Sara Teasdale (1884–1933)

When I Heard the Learn'd Astronomer

When I heard the learn'd astronomer,
When the proofs, the figures, were ranged in columns
    before me,
When I was shown the charts and diagrams, to add,
    divide, and measure them,
When I sitting heard the astronomer where he
    lectured with much applause in the lecture-room,
How soon unaccountable I became tired and sick,
Till rising and gliding out I wander'd off by myself,
In the mystical moist night-air, and from time to time,
Look'd up in perfect silence at the stars.

Walt Whitman (1819–1892)

Song of Apollo

The sleepless Hours who watch me as I lie
    Curtained with star-enwoven tapestries
From the broad moonlight of the open sky,
    Fanning the busy dreams from my dim eyes, –
Waken me when their mother, the grey Dawn,
Tells them that dreams and that the moon is gone.

Then I arise; and climbing Heaven's blue dome,
    I walk over the mountains and the waves,
Leaving my robe upon the ocean foam;
    My footsteps pave the clouds with fire; the caves
Are filled with my bright presence, and the air
Leaves the green Earth to my embraces bare.

The sunbeams are my shafts with which I kill
    Deceit, that loves the night and fears the day;
All men who do, or even imagine ill
    Fly me; and from the glory of my ray
Good minds and open actions take new might,
Until diminished by the reign of night.

I feed the clouds, the rainbows and the flowers
    With their aethereal colours; the moon's globe
And the pure stars in their eternal bowers
    Are cinctured with my power as with a robe;
Whatever lamps on Earth or Heaven may shine
Are portions of one spirit; which is mine.

I stand at noon upon the peak of Heaven;
    Then with unwilling steps, I linger down

Into the clouds of the Atlantic even;
  For grief that I depart they weep and frown –
What look is more delightful, than the smile
With which I soothe them from the Western isle?

I am the eye with which the Universe
  Beholds itself, and knows it is divine;
All harmony of instrument and verse,
  All prophecy and medicine are mine,
All light of art or nature: – to my song
Victory and praise, in its own right, belong.

Percy Bysshe Shelley (1792–1822)

He Wishes for the Cloths of Heaven

Had I the heavens' embroidered cloths,
Enwrought with golden and silver light,
The blue and the dim and the dark cloths
Of night and light and the half-light,
I would spread the cloths under your feet:
But I, being poor, have only my dreams;
I have spread my dreams under your feet;
Tread softly because you tread on my dreams.

W. B. Yeats (1865–1939)

On the South Downs

Over the downs there were birds flying,
  Far off glittered the sea,
And toward the north the weald of Sussex
  Lay like a kingdom under me.

I was happier than the larks
  That nest on the downs and sing to the sky –
Over the downs the birds flying
  Were not so happy as I.

It was not you, though you were near,
  Though you were good to hear and see,
It was not earth, it was not heaven,
  It was myself that sang in me.

Sara Teasdale (1884–1933)

The Windhover

To Christ our Lord

I caught this morning morning's minion, king-
    dom of daylight's dauphin, dapple-dawn-drawn
        Falcon, in his riding
    Of the rolling level underneath him steady air,
        and striding
High there, how he rung upon the rein of a wimpling
    wing
In his ecstasy! then off, off forth on swing,
    As a skate's heel sweeps smooth on a bow-bend:
        the hurl and gliding
    Rebuffed the big wind. My heart in hiding
Stirred for a bird, – the achieve of, the mastery of the
    thing!

Brute beauty and valour and act, oh, air, pride,
    plume, here
    Buckle! AND the fire that breaks from thee then, a
        billion
Times told lovelier, more dangerous, O my chevalier!

No wonder of it: shéer plód makes plough down sillion
Shine, and blue-bleak embers, ah my dear,
    Fall, gall themselves, and gash gold-vermilion.

Gerard Manley Hopkins (1844–1889)

from Childe Harold's Pilgrimage

There is a pleasure in the pathless woods,
There is a rapture on the lonely shore,
There is society, where none intrudes,
By the deep Sea, and music in its roar:
I love not Man the less, but Nature more,
From these our interviews, in which I steal
From all I may be, or have been before,
To mingle with the Universe, and feel
What I can ne'er express, yet cannot all conceal.

George Gordon, Lord Byron (1788–1824)

Where Go the Boats?

Dark brown is the river,
    Golden is the sand.
It flows along for ever,
    With trees on either hand.

Green leaves a-floating,
    Castles of the foam,
Boats of mine a-boating –
    Where will all come home?

On goes the river
    And out past the mill,
Away down the valley,
    Away down the hill.

Away down the river,
    A hundred miles or more,
Other little children
    Shall bring my boats ashore.

Robert Louis Stevenson (1850–1894)

A Strip of Blue

I do not own an inch of land,
    But all I see is mine,—
The orchard and the mowing fields,
    The lawns and gardens fine.
The winds my tax-collectors are,
    They bring me tithes divine,—
Wild scents and subtle essences,
    A tribute rare and free;
And, more magnificent than all,
    My window keeps for me
A glimpse of blue immensity,—
    A little strip of sea.

Richer am I than he who owns
    Great fleets and argosies;
I have a share in every ship
    Won by the inland breeze,
To loiter on yon airy road
    Above the apple-trees,
I freight them with my untold dreams;
    Each bears my own picked crew,
And nobler cargoes wait for them
    Than ever India knew,—
My ships that sail into the East
    Across that outlet blue.

Sometimes they seem like living shapes,—
    The people of the sky,—
Guests in white raiment coming down
    From heaven, which is close by,

I call them by familiar names,
    As one by one draws nigh,
So white, so light, so spirit-like,
    From violet mists they bloom!
The aching wastes of the unknown
    Are half reclaimed from gloom,
Since on life's hospitable sea
    All souls find sailing-room.

The ocean grows a weariness
    With nothing else in sight;
Its east and west, its north and south,
    Spread out from morn till night;
We miss the warm, caressing shore,
    Its brooding shade and light.

Lucy Larcom (1824–1893)

Exultation is in the Going

Exultation is in the going
Of an inland soul to sea,
Past the houses—past the headlands—
Into deep Eternity—

Bred as we, among the mountains,
Can the sailor understand
The divine intoxication
Of the first league out from land?

Emily Dickinson (1830–1886)

The Winds of Fate

One ship drives east and another drives west
    With the selfsame winds that blow.
        'Tis the set of the sails
        And not of the gales
      Which tells us the way to go.

Like the winds of the sea are the ways of fate,
    As we voyage along through life,
        'Tis the set of a soul
        That decides its goal,
      And not the calm or the strife

Ella Wheeler Wilcox (1850–1919)

Emigravit

With sails full set, the ship her anchor weighs.
Strange names shine out beneath her figure head
What glad farewells with eager eyes are said!
What cheer for him who goes, and him who stays!
Fair skies, rich lands, new homes, and untried days
Some go to seek: the rest but wait instead,
Watching the way wherein their comrades led,
Until the next stanch ship her flag doth raise.
Who knows what myriad colonies there are
Of fanest fields, and rich, undreamed-of gains
Thick planted in the distant shining plains
Which we call sky because they lie so far?
Oh, write of me, not "Died in bitter pains,"
But "Emigrated to another star!"

Helen Hunt Jackson (1830–1885)

PEACE AND CONSOLATION

Rest and Be Thankful!

At the head of Glencoe

Doubling and doubling with laborious walk,
Who, that has gained at length the wished-for Height,
This brief, this simple wayside Call can slight,
And rests not thankful? Whether cheered by talk
With some loved friend, or by the unseen hawk
Whistling to clouds and sky-born streams, that shine
At the sun's outbreak, as with light divine,
Ere they descend to nourish root and stalk
Of valley flowers. Nor, while the limbs repose,
Will we forget that, as the fowl can keep
Absolute stillness, poised aloft in air,
And fishes front, unmoved, the torrent's sweep, –
So may the Soul, through powers that Faith bestows,
Win rest, and ease, and peace, with bliss that Angels
    share.

William Wordsworth (1770–1850)

After great pain, a formal feeling comes –

After great pain, a formal feeling comes –
The Nerves sit ceremonious, like Tombs –
The stiff Heart questions was it He, that bore,
And Yesterday, or Centuries before?

The Feet, mechanical go round –
Of Ground, or Air, or Ought –
A Wooden way
Regardless grown,
A Quartz contentment, like a stone –

This is the Hour of Lead –
Remembered, if outlived,
As Freezing persons, recollect the snow –
First – Chill – then Stupor – then the letting go –

Emily Dickinson (1830–1886)

When the Heart is Hard

When the heart is hard and parched up, come upon
    me with a shower of mercy.
When grace is lost from life, come with a burst of song.
When tumultuous work raises its din on all sides
    shutting me out from beyond, come to me, my
    lord of silence, with thy peace and rest.
When my beggarly heart sits crouched, shut up in a
    corner, break open the door, my king, and come
    with the ceremony of a king.
When desire blinds the mind with delusion and dust,
    O thou holy one, thou wakeful, come with thy
    light and thy thunder.

Rabindranath Tagore (1861–1941)

Ode on Solitude

Happy the man, whose wish and care
    A few paternal acres bound,
Content to breathe his native air
      In his own ground.

Whose herds with milk, whose fields with bread,
    Whose flocks supply him with attire,
Whose trees in summer yield him shade,
      In winter fire.

Blest, who can unconcern'dly find
    Hours, days, and years slide soft away,
In health of body, peace of mind,
      Quiet by day.

Sound sleep by night; study and ease,
    Together mixt; sweet recreation:
And innocence, which most does please
      With meditation.

Thus let me live, unseen, unknown,
    Thus unlamented let me die,
Steal from the world, and not a stone
      Tell where I lie.

Alexander Pope (1688–1744)

'I'm thankful that my life doth not deceive'

I'm thankful that my life doth not deceive
Itself with a low loftiness, half height,
And think it soars when still it dip its way
Beneath the clouds on noiseless pinion
Like the crow or owl, but it doth know
The full extent of all its trivialness,
Compared with the splendid heights above.

    See how it waits to watch the mail come in
While 'hind its back *the sun goes out perchance.*
And yet their lumbering cart brings me no word
Not one scrawled leaf such as my neighbors get
To cheer them with the slight events forsooth
Faint ups and downs of their far distant friends
And now tis passed. What next? See the long train
Of teams wreathed in dust, their atmosphere;
Shall I attend until the last is passed?
Else why these ears that hear the leader's bells
Or eyes that link me in procession.
But hark! the drowsy day has done its task,
Far in yon hazy field where stands a barn
Unanxious hens improve the sultry hour
And with contented voice now brag their deed –
A new laid egg – Now let the day decline –
They'll lay another by tomorrow's sun.

Henry David Thoreau (1817–1862)

Ode to Tranquillity

Tranquillity! thou better name
Than all the family of Fame!
Thou ne'er wilt leave my riper age
To low intrigue, or factious rage;
For oh! dear child of thoughtful Truth,
To thee I gave my early youth,
And left the bark, and blest the steadfast shore,
Ere yet the tempest rose and scared me with its roar.

Who late and lingering seeks thy shrine,
On him but seldom, Power divine,
Thy spirit rests! Satiety
And Sloth, poor counterfeits of thee,
Mock the tired worldling. Idle Hope
And dire Remembrance interlope,
To vex the feverish slumbers of the mind:
The bubble floats before, the spectre stalks behind.

But me thy gentle hand will lead
At morning through the accustomed mead;
And in the sultry summer's heat
Will build me up a mossy seat;
And when the gust of Autumn crowds,
And breaks the busy moonlight clouds,
Thou best the thought canst raise, the heart attune,
Light as the busy clouds, calm as the gliding moon.

The feeling heart, the searching soul,
To thee I dedicate the whole!
And while within myself I trace
The greatness of some future race,
   Aloof with hermit-eye I scan
   The present works of present man –
A wild and dream-like trade of blood and guile,
Too foolish for a tear, too wicked for a smile!

Samuel Taylor Coleridge (1772–1834)

Home, Sweet Home!

'Mid pleasures and palaces though we may roam,
Be it ever so humble, there's no place like home
A charm from the sky seems to hallow us there,
Which, seek through the world, is ne'er met with
elsewhere.
        Home! sweet home!
        There's no place like home!

An exile from home, splendour dazzles in vain!
Oh! give me my lowly thatch'd cottage again!
The birds singing gaily that came at my call,
Give me them, with the peace of mind DEARER
    than all!
        Home! sweet home!
        There's no place like home!

John Howard Payne (1791–1852)

St Martin's Summer

As swallows turning backward
    When half-way o'er the sea,
At one word's trumpet summons
    They came again to me –
The hopes I had forgotten
    Came back again to me.

I know not which to credit,
    O lady of my heart!
Your eyes that bade me linger,
    Your words that bade us part –
I know not which to credit,
    My reason or my heart.

But be my hopes rewarded,
    Or be they but in vain,
I have dreamed a golden vision,
    I have gathered in the grain –
I have dreamed a golden vision,
    I have not lived in vain.

Robert Louis Stevenson (1850–1894)

Moonlit Apples

At the top of the house the apples are laid in rows,
And the skylight lets the moonlight in, and those
Apples are deep-sea apples of green. There goes
    A cloud on the moon in the autumn night.

A mouse in the wainscot scratches, and scratches, and
    then
There is no sound at the top of the house of men
Or mice; and the cloud is blown, and the moon again
    Dapples the apples with deep-sea light.

They are lying in rows there, under the gloomy beams;
On the sagging floor; they gather the silver streams
Out of the moon, those moonlit apples of dreams,
    And quiet is the steep stair under.

In the corridors under there is nothing but sleep.
And stiller than ever on orchard boughs they keep
Tryst with the moon, and deep is the silence, deep
    On the moon-washed apples of wonder.

John Drinkwater (1882–1937)

The Loom of Time

Man's life is laid in the loom of time
    To pattern he does not see,
While the weavers work and the shuttles fly
    Till the dawn of eternity.

Some shuttles are filled with silver threads
    And some with threads of gold,
While often but the darker hues
    Are all that they may hold.

But the weaver watches with skilful eye
    Each shuttle fly to and fro,
And sees the pattern so deftly wrought
    As the loom moves sure and slow.

God surely planned the pattern:
    Each thread, the dark and fair,
Is chosen by His master skill
    And placed in the web with care.

He only knows its beauty,
    And guides the shuttles which hold
The threads so unattractive,
    As well as the threads of gold.

Not till each loom is silent,
    And the shuttles cease to fly,
Shall God reveal the pattern
    And explain the reason why

The dark threads were as needful
    In the weaver's skilful hand
As the threads of gold and silver
    For the pattern which He planned.

                                Anon.

Thanks in Old Age

Thanks in old age – thanks ere I go,
For health, the midday sun, the impalpable
    air – for life, mere life,
For precious ever-lingering memories, (of you
    my mother dear – you, father – you, brothers,
    sisters, friends,)
For all my days – not those of peace alone – the
    days of war the same,
For gentle words, caresses, gifts from foreign lands,
For shelter, wine and meat – for sweet appreciation,
(You distant, dim unknown – or young or
    old –countless, unspecified, readers belov'd,
We never met, and ne'er shall meet – and yet
    our souls embrace, long, close and long;)
For beings, groups, love, deeds, words, books – for
    colors, forms,
For all the brave strong men – devoted, hardy
    men – who've forward sprung in freedom's help,
    all years, all lands,
For braver, stronger, more devoted men – (a
    special laurel ere I go, to life's war's chosen ones,
The cannoneers of song and thought – the
    great artillerists– the foremost leaders,
    captains of the soul:)
As soldier from an ended war return'd– As traveler
    out of myriads, to the long procession retrospective,
Thanks – joyful thanks! –a soldier's, traveler's thanks.

Walt Whitman (1819–1892)

Beautiful Old Age

It ought to be lovely to be old
to be full of the peace that comes of experience
and wrinkled ripe fulfilment.

The wrinkled smile of completeness that follows a life
lived undaunted and unsoured with accepted lies.
If people lived without accepting lies
they would ripen like apples, and be scented like
    pippins
in their old age.

Soothing, old people should be, like apples
when one is tired of love.
Fragrant like yellowing leaves, and dim with the soft
stillness and satisfaction of autumn.

And a girl should say:
It must be wonderful to live and grow old.
Look at my mother, how rich and still she is! –

And a young man should think: By Jove
my father has faced all weathers, but it's been a life! –

D. H. Lawrence (1885–1930)

So Be My Passing

A late lark twitters from the quiet skies
And from the west,
Where the sun, his day's work ended,
Lingers as in content,
There falls on the old, gray city
An influence luminous and serene,
A shining peace.

The smoke ascends
In a rosy-and-golden haze. The spires
Shine and are changed. In the valley
Shadows rise. The lark sings on. The sun,
Closing his benediction,
Sinks, and the darkening air
Thrills with a sense of the triumphing night –
Night with her train of stars
And her great gift of sleep.

So be my passing!
My task accomplish'd and the long day done,
My wages taken, and in my heart
Some late lark singing,
Let me be gather'd to the quiet west,
The sundown splendid and serene,
Death.

W. E. Henley (1849–1903)

Index of Poets

Index of Titles

Index of First Lines